HOMEMADE SHRINE

By: Danii Jasmine

Copyright © 2024 by Danii Jasmine.

All rights reserved.

No part of this publication may be reproduced, distributed, or transmitted in any form or by any means, including photocopying, recording, or other electronic or mechanical methods, without the prior written permission of the publisher, except in the case of brief quotations embodied in critical reviews and certain other noncommercial uses permitted by copyright law. For permission requests, contact beerboleyn@gmail.com.

Book Cover by Danii Jasmine
Illustrations/Scrapbook Art by Brooklyn Whitney (Instagram: @ideal_gutter)

www.DaniiJasmine.com

I'd like to thank AAWP, Recent Work Press and Ink Drop Publishers for publishing the poems "Brandy Melville" & "Recollection Before A Storm" featured in this collection respectively.

for A.G.
you were once everything
turned to nothing.

a shrine to a different part of my life. . .

POEMS

1. SUNSHINELATER — 2
2. DAYLIGHT/MOONLIGHT — 7
3. WILDFIRE — 11
4. DEPRESS DAYDREAM — 16
5. INEVITABLE KARMA — 19
6. BRANDY MELVILLE — 21
7. THE REASON — 25
8. ANGEL ARROWHEAD HIGHWAY — 26
9. HONEY'S BEEN MISSING! — 31
10. THE STARS ARE ALREADY DEAD FROM THIS POINT OF VIEW — 33
11. BEER-BOLEYN — 38
12. THE COMMON EMIGRANT — 40
13. SUGAR WINGS — 44
14. STRAWBERRIES & CREAM — 46
15. RECOLLECTION BEFORE A STORM — 53
16. BETTER TO SLEEP — 58
17. VIDEO FREAK — 62
18. SUNLIGHT EATER — 67
19. YOU'RE NEEDLE — 71
20. THE CHERRY PIT — 75
21. HOSPITAL DRUGS — 77
22. DEADEND — 81
23. FOREIGN GODS — 85

♡SUNSHINELATER♡

while drifting into unconsciousness to escape
the inevitable sting of the
cold air
i felt your presence
within a dreaming building again—
it was a hotel for the grieving—
stuck in the middle of my sleep. . .

when i was awake
it was to pinks & blues preluding the oncoming dark
& what was left
of the afternoon's vacant breezes
drifted through my shutters carrying with them
a smell of death & drying detergent
stirring up a now-rotten nostalgia-trip within my
heart-beaten head.

they felt like fake memories from
childhood's own front lawn
taking a breath
—strawberry-scented tea
& flower-embroidered pillowcases—
an eerie
other-worldly
sense of peace.

outside—
empty suburban houses
sitting in the approaching
eve
posed as momentary headstones
haunted by the fading ghosts of
rose-tinted reveries
—all delusional daydreams—

the sunset spilled over & collapsed
onto the empty sidewalk

with a silent thud of footsteps—
in its final desperation
—earth was meeting the stars
—*& it meant nothing to me too*
—living in a windowless mind because
you were far better than the near-apocalyptic sky.

the oven-light posed as new life instead—
as what remained of the sun still crept slowly
across the cold kitchen floor
towards me
—*near death*—
as the familiar framed photographs of a glass-cased
past grew pitch-dark—
birthday candles from two-weeks ago
stayed in the sink
& rooms in my dusty dollhouse
continued to form their own clockwork heartbeats.

earlier—
you had hated the song that reminded me of you
& exclaimed it was another *xanax night*—
you know you could make the dirt inside of me bloom
your own anti-depressant daydream
without fight.

"how to cope"
i wondered
as i contemplated turning my blood
with another screwdriver
—*outside*
the crickets fell into the stomach
of the once sun-baked lawn—
& i was ever pacing back & forth
while the foreign tunes you had sent me
screamed.

those familiar slaughterhouse fumes

soon floated back into my quiet room
by dusk—
going straight to the head-hazy
sowing familiar doubts within my brain
that strayed far from fair.

—while drifting right back into unconsciousness
to escape screaming recollection
the only promise of light now floated upon the
horizon—
but it won't dig its way deep enough
into my skin
to break this same old reverie
you like to haunt me in—

5

—it keeps trying. . .

perfection
never felt so pure over phone lines, around the world
way around, where you send your winter up there,
summer down here songs, just for you and me...

... i'm fucked.

♡DAYLIGHT/MOONLIGHT♡

I.

at last
an autumn morning
& the smell of smoke
fills suburbia
from another
man-made tragedy—
claustrophobic traffic
& invasive voices of loved ones
really can weigh down
the distant catcalls of the crows—
—the days belong to us—
while the cats hide under our cars
& the cicadas call out to each other
from their large leafy palaces
in morse code—
the wind is vengeful
all the while—
retaliation is strong
when done right—
a construction fence collapses
under its pressure onto a pedestrian pathway—
cold air bites at the flesh—
large distant cranes
are backlit in the sun
overshadowing a thriving park—
& *we're* all painted as evil—
suppressed—
perverted
destructive
depressed

...*& lost*
by *sundown*.

II.

it's dead outside
just after twilight—
distant
twinkling streetlights
lightly litter *nature's dark—*
hidden best by leaves
that are disturbed occasionally
by the now
softer breeze—
firefly beams drive home
to loved ones and
delusional safety—
all the front doors
now closed on the
curious—
planes pose as moving stars
in the distance—
some
    are
        faster
            than others
but their games are meaningless—
the night belongs
to the hedonistic creatures—
outside
with the blood-sucking insects—
the moths search
for *neon delight—*
smaller bugs on the insect food-chain
suicide dive into my red wine
& *i'm the one forced into guilt*
wondering what drowning

9

in pure indulgence
may feel like—
staring across at the dirt ditch
littered with construction—
at last painted black
& still attempting
to build *nature's grave—*
the only other sign of human life
is a distant fading flashlight
amid the black—
just for two seconds
no more—
lost for good among
the creatures of the night.

I picked some oleander flowers near that abandoned house with intention of pressing them. I found out they were potentially poisonous and reluctantly threw them in the trash. Feels like I killed them. I should have kept them.
Now dead, corrupt, decaying and unwanted, <u>used, discarded, no longer "pretty"</u>

♡WILDFIRE♡

it was sweet hell
when i would visit
your daydream's golden doors
—the secret place past the decorative roses & vines
& the rolling hills in *supernatural mist*
—the place sitting on the edge
of what was left of our romanticised world
that could only breathe inside my head.

under the heat
& the melting christmas lights
hanging still in the summer sun
these short garden dreams of mine
were preparing me
for a hard-cut change—
the park down the road
near the little cemetery
& far outside the basement brain
where i used to talk to you
had once housed only *loving reveries*
but was too soon set ablaze
by troubled arsonists
& now grows demons like dandelions
in the dead of sleep.

the mind is nothing but an overgrown manor of
debauchery
really—
the black garden that grows in mine
from the flood you had sent to calm the flame
you started there
only brought up possessive vines
that entwined with my veins & squeezed them *too tight*
dragging me further into a deranged state of

12

'just fine'
from your imagined will alone.

—you talk like a slot machine—
our hedonistic nature
should have been corrected
with a rusty flamethrower years ago
but
what i miss is your electric security in the air
—what a miss too far to be near
—from what i hear you're a mess over there
you're just hanging by a thread. . .

you're a chemical-infused
pink-peony-wet-dream
that keeps re-running—
so wide awake
something had to break—
have you seen the news lately?
the world is burning on both ends now
for

              you

&
me
—two flames selfishly trying to be one
against all odds
—they could build hedonistic cities upon
our lustful parasites alone
that turn to ash just as quickly.

my heart still opens up
to the idea of having yours
like poison oleander
in my own smoking air
far from *the dreaming tree*—
all of your words are turned too ethereal
in the bad weather of my mind
forcing me onto the bathroom floor whenever
they say *"no."*

13

save me instead & give me those quiet
eerily peaceful
& bloodless nights
still tainted with the smell of wildfires
on coming winter breezes
but now with *lively evacuations—*
you say *"fuck California"*
but i dream to escape to your imagined
as pretty sea salt state *only*.

"Destroyed in Love"

Poem # 26. May 25th, 2018

Now, I want to drown, but not in the ocean.
I want to drown in the rose water and honey kisses.
Deep down, in the garden, i'll want to gorge out of my gord, with sweetness and indulgences, until I feel wonderfully sick.
I want to destroy myself with only the sweet things now, only the healthy and not so bleak.
I want to destroy myself in love

♡List #1♡
Things That Tend to Start a Fire
Deep Within You

1. _____
_____
_____
_____

2. _____
_____
_____
_____

3. _____
_____
_____
_____

4. _____
_____
_____
_____

5. _____
_____
_____
_____

♡DEPRESS DAYDREAM♡

there's the white rabbit
touring the cemetery hedge maze
that lives next to your little depression-daydream
back on your childhood street—
sipped frozen milk
through a flower-print straw
in the backyard
of your reveried
as happy family barbecue by the seaview—
sinister stares invisible—
sitting in laps
& inhaling the flesh-biting
dusty home-video air too—
you give your strawberry-drenched drink to me
& make a face—
it seems you play pretend with happiness far better
in alternate reality—
less lonely—
your bright future
now nothing but a black-hole of *young grief.*

& harsh consciousness is fingering tired eyes
& never entirely erasing the *downer-dazing-feeling*—
there's a distant light in your green irises
that can only be found in some imaginary memory
of a winter barbecue
sunday evening
pre-death daydream—

17

but it's far warmer

trapped in love regret.

he needs something
to take the edge off
Let it be me.
use me.
I love the feeling.

♡INEVITABLE KARMA♡

i didn't want to be
your inevitable karma
but all your salvation
—*sort of happy ever after*—
you weren't that shooting star
that i wanted—
you were the satellite
still hidden deep down in the darkness
—now i'm burning your bridge down
so i can separate our ideals
& stop fantasising about when i'll drown—
i'm halting all those words—
i promise to never write again
 about your stars or your *ctv blues*—
i won't make a sound—
      i won't even pretend.

♡BRANDY MELVILLE♡

you had sent me *'Tomorrow's Gone'* amid an *All-American valentine's day*
as the morning light crept across the ceiling like an approaching predator
once again
—you were trying to tell me something new & sweet—
sweet needle-tip slick & inhaling honey—
penetrating the brain that had coloured it rose—
i was yours & you
were kind of mine. . .

just a little more therapy before it turns pitch dark—
i wrote five paragraphs about neglect
& emotional rollercoasters without the thrill
& about *you*
still
no one on the forum knew how to help—turns out i couldn't
even take back the words.

i don't recognise myself anymore—
in these hazy days i'm worried the people around me don't either
or that they now recognise & have warmed to this resigned
sad version far more
& to change for the better would be too much of a shock.

i'll be silently idolising all the other sad-suffered drunks
who are still beautiful
& bound to get wet
wasting away in the fake-light of a tipped vodka bottle—prettily
poisoned over the years
—every day will scream nostalgia
but in a negative way

—tainted blood fuels future buzzed evenings
& self-loathing is ever the *adult theme.*

& *you*—the right-leaning cheap date—*heaven's sweet fallen mistake*—
angel eyes from another time & place that always remain exactly
the same
—while it decays & dictates
your diamond basement mind absorbs worlds—
if i could ever hurt you
my adoration would be your shame
—you star in my ice-cold midnight dreams of
car crashes
lonely graves
& hospital beds
—it seems you're not safe even in my unconscious head.

8 o'clock
steam rising from the drain—unexpected breakdowns in the shower
& dressing for a night-drive date drunken in a dream
—happiness is booze & a best friend for a lover
—hitchhiking in the lonely night
while a cold jasmine assaulted breeze slips down throats
& straight up to lovesick heads at the speed of light
—laying out picnic blankets
in the blackness of the neighbourhood park
while you show off your glock—hold me down flat & rough
whilst making love.

we'll pass by the local longing that emanates
from the abandoned house bordering the traffic
& ignore the long-buried cry for lonesome contentment instead
—i'll lean my heavy head on reverie's shoulder
because the brain is petitioning a need for self-love through
metaphor
that only harms more than it helps.

& in reality. . .
there are circle spells of fireballs & southern comfort
still i'm far from written off—
truth or dare where the questions not so elegantly
deep dive for the hell of it
still i'm far from elated—
turns out you floated exclusively on acid & stayed in touch with
mary-jane
—breaking expensive bass guitars just for fun & lighting morrison
wannabes on fire
supposedly by accident
while pretending to *like* music. . .

at the dawn of my sick tired monday—*your slow depressive sunday*
you'll take your countless pills & regretfully spend your hard-earned
money
on *Brandy Melville*
—i'll drink till 4 a.m. again & find comfort in lonesome pretend
because this is the only way to live in love as far as i can tell.

Just last Saturday, ▬▬▬ had emailed me out of nowhere, which was exciting. He asked how the begginnings of winter were for me, and told me "I had a elaborate dream that starred you it was full of dream details that I always find odd, being they always ring true. Anyway."

You're like small talk about the weather
I'm abandoned and hollow inside
A fire is igniting within my ribcage,
it's hurting, it's killing, it's bitter.
and like insects gnawing on brittle bones
teeth scraping back across hard, cold regret
You're like the weather

♡THE REASON♡

we're all boring in hindsight of human restlessness—
three years lie down mother eternity
& woos her ten times over
before painting her homage & forgetting about her
in the cathedral of
stereotypical masterpieces—
romantic is a creative mind blindly pinning you
in its pitch-black basement
for a moment or two
through the guise of something *new & life affirming*
like motorcycles skidding on the edges
of familiar highway cliff-sides
& jumping out of airplanes
—*you're the reason this is happening*—
we were exactly the same but maybe that's not for the best—
early morning brain-freezes
can only be warmed by late buses' teases
with scheduled fantasy trips
a pleasant dream of the past
that lasts between the hours
of a sad insomniac's sleep—
bitter is the months on months—distant is the humble days
of sweet daydreams in makeshift garden settings
to music
video & tv framings—these things hit in phases
& this one is now repeating
& dreaming of bleeding. . .

♡ANGEL ARROWHEAD HIGHWAY♡

//

yet another summer high in the 40s
—it's the befouled kind of heat that *hangs dead*
—i'm stuck in this brand new desert fever dream
from the '90s
& in here
there's always something wrong with the rain.

my hung-heart had zapped & sparked as it died
for a 2nd time
covered in the dead ravenous insects from the past
that refused to decay along with it.

no longer sticky & sweet
the heart did weep
& my vision blurred & sparkled in your hotbox
while i listened to your shaky
      colourful
      complaints
—it seems my skull
  your black-tinted glass
& *melted ac*
failed to shelter my reeling brain from the damned
repeating summer heat.

your unconscious self smiles so sweet-*sleazily*
—the image alone sticks & seeps like melted honey
overflowing my brain
—this perverse ghost manifests
as a crystal-clear vision
drifting amid dead space reveries

playing the role of the disgusting degenerate side of your
double-life mind
& mine
—he has me beaming brighter
than desert shrine candles & epileptic neon signs.

you are earth's sweet self-destruction
that i've bottled & bathed in just to shed
the beating sun off of my sensitive flesh
—but my brain is ever for lease for your crooked ghost to
haunt & douse in kerosene.

your mind is the solid gold library within heaven's halls
meeting all of las vegas in a tacky snow globe—
instead of the heart now
your brain has taken on the chore of beating you
senseless
right down to the floor
—it's too familiar a feeling to take.

*yet the desert eventually always falls into the stomach of
the staten island river—*
the overbearing voice of my past
never fails
to carry over & drown out the heat
—his words forcing me back to why
i'm borrowing half-measure happiness
from these hapless daydreams
—*the real road to nowhere*
saying goodbye to reality's pointless schemes. . .

pretty lightning glow
projected on the black motel screen—
outside flowers twist & grow under glowing signs
by the almost imaginary-straight-shooting-star-highway
—channel 34 beams from the tv
—a re-run of a skit from another life.

28

i don't know where i'm going
but i'm slowly outrunning the humidity
& the bitter taste of sea salt on my tongue
—*but where oh where*
—where is your own repellent head
if not on me now
midnight to lonely midnight instead?

\\

♡List #2♡
Things (or People) You Detest To Love

1. _____
   _____
   _____
   _____

2. _____
   _____
   _____
   _____

3. _____
   _____
   _____
   _____

4. _____
   _____
   _____
   _____

5. _____
   _____
   _____
   _____

♡*HONEY'S BEEN MISSING!*♡

the unorthodox dream boat
is a critic & a cynic—
his mind is repellent
leaking out all of his clever
& dismal opinions—
but oh—*he's a knockout!*
an unconventional
modern day vision.

well Honey's been missing
—*missing out on all the loving.*

let's not talk of what
i've been reduced to—
dimwit alley bars
& the phobic discos—
modern day dating—
serving all the unruly hands
& all revealing little sickos
& in the meantime
i've just been
working up the blood to
turn on the taboo
past-present charm
& it's all for *you.*

yes cos' *Honey's been a-missing*
& Honey's been *itching*
—missing out on all the loving
you've just been waiting for it to *hit me.*

& well *Honey's a knockout!*
oh—he's the unorthodox dream boat—
setting up all the right notes—

winning me over with all of his talk—
talk of the inevitable—
the daily endless
death-wish bragging.

yes Honey's a cynic—
pessimistic in the right way—
he's far too intelligent
to continue living amid
this detestable new age.

Honey's the modern day—
just another modern day vision
who daydreams endlessly
about the end of his existence.

hell he's a visionary—
dead deep inside with past endeavours—
shrouded in very rundown
evident misery insistence!

but still i believe
he's far *lovelier*
than all the other boys & all their bitches.

♡THE STARS ARE ALREADY DEAD FROM THIS POINT OF VIEW♡

raw & freezing
—mean-streak
—an ache my heart dreams up *for some reason*
—open-shell
—*broken-apart-freak*
—honey-nest
—bitter-hell
—blood & honey
—pretend love spells-*the figurative kind*
—*pretty creep*
—night music
—dismay with my future grave
—night air un-assaulted by death
because my heart is home in a jar
pumping formaldehyde
& you say you're dying
but like a star
drinking through a straw
snorting up *diamond dust*
—force-fed images in the sky
drug it whenever waking up *is a chore*
—*better than acid*
—tea when the bar is dry
—dreams are strange company to keep
—i only play as prey because it's the
mind's *favourite* fucked-off dream
—negative on a sunny day
—tropical vodka lapping up the dirt
—falling in love with week-long rain that leads to floods
—greater disasters than what's happening in my brain

—blood boiling
—*writer's block is a lie*
unhealthy distractions stake their claim
—pretending it's well-earned bitterness
—fearing the peers with sheep brains
—*fearing the inevitable blame*
—stuck in something like *tv schedules*
—hive-mind
sparking in the rain
—eaten alive by cinnamon & year-round wildfires
—untouchable skin
pale & paper-thin
—the paper doll that detests *fun*
—i feel like a ghost any day
—anger management is blank staring into an abyss
& when i hear your voice it places me into a faraway coma
all over again
—valley of death
—masturbatory sigil charge-up for fun
—carousel candle for warmth
—drunk cigarettes
—raw-bitten lips
—hot wax stuck in hair
—*fake memories*
—white lies i inject
—fake safe space
—escaping inside from the bizarre story
of a past i pretend *isn't mine*
—movie drive-ins & getting lit in alternate realities
the ones with *unrealistic happy endings*
—*ever bored*
—*ever horny*
—*ever sick*
—just a fake flesh & blood wallflower still stuck between
brick. . .

written-off on an unknown date, probably around midnight...

There are intimate joys in being drunk, of course there are, the obvious ones. Yet there are also joys that your conscience won't allow you to pursue sober because it holds too much dignity, or too much pain. Booze cuts a brain into pieces, each piece able to filter out the worries, feelings and reality of the other. You can enjoy guilty pleasures confidently whilst drunk, the brain at last is so disconnected from itself and wholly hedonistic. Looking to excite itself, push boundaries, destroy itself... Different voices speak from it, all now able to shut each other out. You get to be the God that chooses which one to listen to, which one to give life to. To indulge in... Writing drunk is a free adventure into the unknown, the exciting, uncaring road less travelled, producing near psychotic magic. I'd love to write about time machines and lovers based off of romantic ideas of fake people. Maybe write a time I never got to know, feelings I'll never properly experience. Moments tucked away and wrapped up lovingly only within the brain - *fantasy housing* - longing fake lovers entwined in jealous dreams that long to tug and hang on heartstrings, to persist and torment lonely Mondays. If only dreams were real instead, well then you would be fighting off archaic demons, serial killers & aliens as part of the very broken, daily routine, there wouldn't just be hyper-sweetened romantic scenes... I digress,

I want to write about a time machine, there's no need for the cheap plots of dreams if I had one. A time machine could get me a certain ring and a padlock, exclusive with theoretical bars on very real suburban windows. I'm supposed to rebel against it, but I want to be a housewife, a willing, loving captive, an endless lover endlessly burning, but for a reason. Who hides her deranged poetry from her husband who practices magick, who lights the house ablaze with scented candles and weird obscure tunes while I practice making it to three squares a day... I want to write about a time machine, some better time, some better place, better people far better at building up their special little personalities, all the same & ever fake. A modern time machine is only the eyes that cannot age. Longing, dead sick of the longing. Perhaps, it could all be avoided with a time machine. Until then, back to the topic of drinking. . .

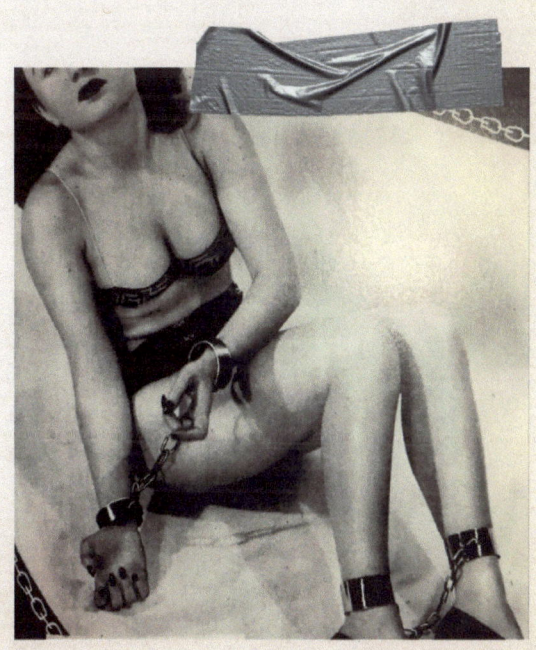

♡BEER-BOLEYN♡

i don't remember the first half of the dream
turns out i never do
it always side-swipes me in the middle of the afternoon
between the bitter lemon & cinnamon daniels'
& as a result i drink a little harder
before class & after.

my head spins when you laugh at my brand-new
bourbon-dazed jokes
& in this funny dream
you somehow came across only *half-condescending*
as you kissed my hand & sent me to the bar
so you could conduct all of your pretentious
self-esteem eating art-meetings
alone.

half-cut—*i'm in too deep*
many offer to save me
but i'm a joke more than a *fling*
—more of a confused excuse
for seduction-induced-debauchery
—preempting another dead-end mood
 for tuesday morning.

out of the loop of your far too adult life
& it's *showing in these unconscious settings*
—you tell me i'd have to pay you to listen to my dreams
—i'm too sensitive for your hypochondriac tendencies
—*you could cut this newfound air with a knife*—
these reveries reek of the tame wish for this relationship
to be put to sleep.

it was like that dream where we ended up having
a thelemic-cult wedding

39

—with a fake smile for home-wrecking
the crowds judged *only me*
as i walked the pretty hilly-aisle
pretending i was anything like *anne boleyn*
on her morning of slaughter
while you casually strolled beside me
drinking beer
—*funnily enough*
days after i had dreamt it
only then had you inexplicably started
slamming down the Coronas you had once detested. . .

♡THE COMMON EMIGRANT♡

an autumn morning
& small wings beat fresh air
to the ground—
recently watered-down daisies
sway steady in their front-lawn home
as they are *fed on*
by the small creature—
the one that is pretty food for the human soul—
filling surrounding heartbeats with
a special sort of desired joy.

midday in april
&
the butterfly drifts through a foreign park of compromises
freely—
barely missing the oncoming activity of children & pets
who now & then
stalk the wings born out of the
seemingly perfect day—
all of the trees & the freshly planted flowers
between the teeth of the sun—
all the rare but lovely human
non-human *harmony.*

all surrounding life stops dead
for two seconds
or so

to stare at the pretty thing & take it as a sign from
something disembodied
& *heavenly—*
turning it into whatever they want it to be—
the butterfly only drifts idly
amongst the daisies in response.

the short space between sunset & the eve
all human life cannot wait
for this sweet space to be
the *new* set of one of their dreams—
warning signs of a storm
soon closes in
forcing all who inhabit to rush *home—*
children scurry to leash pets
yanking them away—
trees sway dangerously—
abandoned—
the butterfly hovers away too from this now lonely part of
the world—
but a large net out of thin-freezing air traps
& halts its short fly home.

yet another autumn morning & small wings are *pinned &
posed—*
the small lemon emigrant is a beautiful stranger
to the collector's *killing jar—*
the overwhelmingly sweet stench of ethyl acetate
drowns out the morning's *icy air*
& douses the butterfly in its wishful beauty.

soon glass-cased and cold—
dead black eyes reflect back a living room—
a television—
sporadic midnight breakdowns & *human promises*—
the pretty creature's forced presence there
fills surrounding heartbeats
with a special sort of desired joy—
now nothing but pretty decor
bought & sold—
whatever you want it to be.

told him that I was sure everyone hated me after I was a drunk, obnoxious idiot who could barely walk. "You're so god damned beautiful, no one will care," He told me

"...you get away with everything" he had said, reffering to "pretty people". Maybe he's right.

I wish my mind would leave me alone

♡SUGAR WINGS♡

i'm dead wings to you
—*garden-sludge heart*
—*paralysis-pincer bait*
—my mind is holding in emotional vomit
—insides are eating their-selves out
—can't leave your golden butterfly cage in the basement
so i'll drink shots in sips under the caked
dusty table
& talk funny to the degenerate
drunken shadows. . .

it's not living when the heart is always *figuratively dying*
—red wine tracing wasted time
through rosy spiderweb veins
—i don't care if my insides are poisoned
as long as the outside stays pretty
—i have a perverse need to be used
—*turn my body into an insect farm.*

sweet *loving* rusty scissors clipping memory—
you have wings with paper-cuts & go missing to silence
a week before your birthday
—*your voice*
harnessed within my indulgent bones
was something i did not choose
—**Christ**
i'm so **sick** of loving you.

my own porcelain wings
were born to now & then

45

anticipate the razor only
but you don't give a fuck & you know that it shows
—hoping now & then that you'll drop your guard
—you'll break pretend
—you'll look at me with fascination again
—*you'll call me 'Sweetness. . .'*

♡STRAWBERRIES & CREAM♡

—deranged lust
—*monday morning*
& you inhale vanilla coated cigarettes
far away
—*freezing smoke in your own cool air*
—so sweet is the forbidden wish
                                          —*that i*
were the smoke in your lungs instead—
heating up your insides
with unrealistic fantasies *only*
the ones we could never really live...

—porn-rotted-brain
—sweet-tooth
i'm gagging upon your imagined as *sweetly-sickening*
decadent
strawberries & cream scent
—i'm tracing your distant frame in past photographs
with heavy-honey-glazed eyes—
my own country's heat injects its perversions
into my rose-thick bloodstream
& the mind subsists annoyingly on
repeating your name.

youth is gun-shyly discovering
"who i truly am"
while something far different
reflects back in your own disconnected eyes
that stay exactly the same regardless of if it's

1991 or 2025
—*youth adores those veiny-vine entwined windows into the long-trashed soul*
—*i'll romanticise you drugging my sweet tea*—
sleepy-sexy-delight
all yours for free!

you probably respond to the porn
in the *afterglow*
—*ever a fan of all the ugly love songs*—
you have a perfect balance
between overly selfish-pretentious &
sweetly modest.

you may think that you're pinned
not quite right—
hanging behind dusty glass & twisting inwards during
silent-killing-summertime
but
you are the brightest & biggest bleak bibliophilic butterfly
whose more than *half* fallen angel
—*love's unorthodox collector's delight!*

you used to remind me
of saturday morning nervous pacing
giddy on the dead lawn
giggling on the brain-sizzling phone
as you described the inside of your filthy head to me
for the first time
—*big eyes rolling*—
but now you remind me solely of razors
& ice-cold shooting pains
like ice-cream numbing veins.

you like to write that suburbia's clichés have their hold on
you now that you're no longer mine
—front lawn murder
on halloween
—the smell of massacred grass
& wet roses in the garden—
you'll perversely spray the trespassers
with sick glee
who attempt to steal away
all of your time-tested generosity.

praying for a white winter to come &
freeze the overbearing sea-salt
—*you'll be careful not to slip & fall*
—*ideas too sweet for your own karma.*

monday morning dazed
& i'm forcing down strawberry-flavoured meclizine pills
—the taste is a disgusting nostalgia trip
like cold lonely days lying in bed
while the mind works like a *merry-go-round*.

i'll forever gag on hate & drool
behind calling you a *'liar'*
but
everlasting *still*
is this lust &
this stone-steel love for you
against every one of my summer's wildfires. . .

♡List #3♡
Private Fantasies of Any Nature...

1. _____
_____
_____
_____
_____

2. _____
_____
_____
_____
_____

3. _____
_____
_____
_____

4. _____
_____
_____
_____

5. _____
_____
_____
_____

more. you kept chuckling and complaining about the awkward,
mundane chatting we continued to keep up, but I fell in
love with every single second of it. i hope you didn't take
notice of my shaky voice
You called me "dear" or "my dear" and my heart went
into a brief panic as it tried desperately to crawl out
of my throat and tried to attempt to attach itself
from its body as it tried to abandon ship, it
was into a sweet moan when you entered my house even was in

I moved back
inside my house
it was empty now
and you must
have sensed it
too. "Now, what you have to
do, is spread your legs for me, a little
wider, that's it, ruh yes, that's it" huff
My tone
changed immediately at the sudden change in
directions, the arousal
would not be real but sex
was instant, and built up by the fact that it was actually
on the phone this time. It got me producing-
I was "he around moaned the name "Tim, huh" and asked if
and turned to be a "cum dump" I moaned "yes" and the
moaning pornstar at his command.
began to
grow breathless as well. He brought up everything
we had talked and fantasised about over email and
messages and   your
was losing my mind. He told me to   voice
Cum and soon the orgasm came upon me as he began
was loud. "There she is," he
my sudden vocal explosion he didn't get to
cum himself it was fine. "phone sex!" he exclaimed "this was a
           god, he really raised me as   rubbed and tried to
nice introduction",
to moan as well. I
breathlessly commented at

voice was delightful and that you can
just through hearing

Commented that
my voice
tell a lot about who

                        god threes   more to come. you
                                   rehearsal but that you might
their voice. What did you find out about me? You called me
        sweeter that days   the second time. When we
   said you had to   each other "bye bye" and hung up,
    go to   the universe,, all the same as
Call again later that
"Sweetness"

♡RECOLLECTION BEFORE A STORM♡

on warm tiles
stirring tea
—outside the clouds are grey flesh sheltering sunshine
veins
& underneath the roof is an internal battle *dead-silent*
cutting deeper past imperfect skin & faded freckles
—*i really do detest the morning routine*—
if you do something nice
more than once then you'll begin to live
like an addict
& you'll spend all your remaining pennies on far better
5-minute memories
—in summer i was a coma-obsessed bitter joke
—memory of that sticky heat still stays overwhelming. . .

across the unruly field
i used to make home movies with friends
& it feels longer than 4 years ago
—the first flirtatious thoughts of mortality consumed me
—wrapping around the brain
—a secret first meeting with affordable poison
floral candles & *a makeshift blade.*

5-minutes away
is a home that's still a set for routine nightmares to play—
a dream museum covered in cobwebs

& unconscious indecision
—full of ghosts that still crave to possess new lovers
& turn them against me in bizarre reveries
& the corner with the same house painted black that still breathes & emanates
something sinister to me.

ten minutes away
atop a makeshift hill
i can't even remember what the entrance looks like
but i remember the walk to school
—lonely in the dead of summer when summer was just as cruel
—dreams of starving-hospital beds & meaner kids & dead insects littering carpets
poisoning my food.

i tend to inspire blind violence
the unspoken kind
rarely acted upon
—christmas 2020
& the novelty village sounds drunk
repeating the same classics
& projecting something perfect & lit-up
to drown out the dripping venom
of the family cooped up with it for far too long.

why did i ever dream about escaping in someone like you?
—forever buried under cement

in the field of regret
—i'm a yearning bad luck charm full of poison
living off of a handful of better days
—not as sweet as all your previous exciting &
high hedonistic fantasies-turned brand new memories
of *me*
    movies
        weed
            & sushi.

the heat hangs dead—
   so i want you instead
—*the sweet pothead*
with redeeming content—
   birthday-candle-
   smoke-inhaling-
      death-wish-
      dream-honey—
you're inadvertently
 undressing me daily—
you're a comfortable dose of your own sweet nostalgia
re-running every morning
—*forever the half-glass optimist & now the distant dream.*

time's the enemy of mother memory
—eventually
familiar voices become far better background noises
—the lingering heat makes friends with the
inevitable *midday-buzz*
& the pounding sun is more involved with your brain

than those fake-fixated relatives are.

sporadic summer rain that briefly comforts & buzzes like a person
—i've come to the conclusion
that i'd rather be a mere background presence within your world instead
of the main focus in my own
—the tempting dreams inviting me to make friends with the rival in the end
but outside of the head
i'm bitter
meek
& nothing ever happens outside
of a rare-bird tragedy
—*life's one convincing strategy*
—in the end
a family is such a fragile roof under reality.

List #46: What 2 think about 2 quieten those nerves...

1. You're so god damned beautiful that no one will care — do anything anything

2. We will all die one day, remember ~~that~~

3. Everyone is scared

4. You can fucking destroy people

you're beautiful, smart, funny
no one will care

No one will love me as much as I them.

♡BETTER TO SLEEP♡

it reeked like a dead garden in the shuttered away kitchen
—the lilies' necks were hung dead past the vase
down with another sundown
—i had left the romantic task of pressing them for far too long.

tangy afternoon air carrying *lola* by *the kinks*—
hummingbirds trying to accompany *ms london*—*your new love*
without voices
—small clusters of insects
born in the sunset
frozen in place
by the cold air drifting up from hose-drenched driveways
—feeding off of clementine & tangerine to the scent of *recycled waves*
—i remember picnics in the gutter as storms closed in—
the fading sun briefly drifting into regretted
open scars
—*like fairy spotlights*—
crawling through wintery leaves like *magic vines*—
new cuts acquired solely from the too soon
freezing flowerbeds. . .

i was dreaming of pinning butterflies again—
freezing something gorgeous that's permanent
—*never to grow mundane*
—trying my hand at pinning & posing in an excuse for weird catharsis.

tired of bleeding & of deceiving optimistic daydreams
—drunk mondays where my own blankets feel far too freezing
—covering-up fresh scars
& standing up straight in the mirror only

—i feel like nothing but the buzzing air around the non-consenting tv screen
—stuck in a loop.

while the trees sway outside of me—loud music downstairs infests the insides of dry walls
—shaking the cobwebs—
a rush of fresh air & sirens in the awakening moment of pure ecstasy
—same old sunrise to sunset dream.

disembodied voice of heaven's gate guides me ten steps down the driveway
    romantically
        tenderly
unrealistically
using your dead winter sighs alone
—strolling through this silent neighbourhood close to 3am longing to smash whiskey bottles against once wet driveways
until the knife stops twisting
—*better to sleep*
& waste away in dreams—nauseous with the realisation that the habit to build homes inside of me
die as hard as this naive feeling. . .

"special"

poem #84: February 18th, 2019

pressed flowers and pinned butterflies
you're not special,
reading a lover's mind and speaking in
eyes,
you're not special,

shooting stars and overwhelming feelings that
it all must be a sign,
you're not special,

your tears, blood and knees on the
bathroom floor, it feels the world targets
only you once again but,
you're not special,

they love you, they choose you, they must
it's written in the stang
you're not special

Name etched into grim stone grey
too soon, a tragedy, never forget, never
forget, they say with a heart
full of tears whilst
you're not special,
rest of the dead they
to ~~suppress~~ you too,

♡List #4♡
Things You Should Face Up To (Even If They Tend To Cut Like A Knife)

1. _____
   _____
   _____
   _____

2. _____
   _____
   _____
   _____

3. _____
   _____
   _____
   _____

4. _____
   _____
   _____
   _____

5. _____
   _____
   _____
   _____

♡VIDEO FREAK♡

i'm visiting your grave today
—i'm bringing fresh daisies
& scars & my new dress
—i'm sitting down in the dirt
& i'm feeling deranged
giggling in front of the final resting place
of the filthy & half-lobotomized
side of your brain
—in a jar
—in the electric-graveyard
on your lost forum for ghosts
a fitting tomb from the '90s
where your fake personality is still dead online
hanging from the ceiling
—i wanted **him** not you
the person you were pretending to be
maybe it's because there's something just as sick
inside of me?
long-buried
i want to be
used
spat-on
collared
caged
a captive
a victim
i'm such a perfect victim that it *scares* me
—eat me alive like the ants
a black ocean of desire
rumbles deep down inside of me
longing to *spill free*
to be a victim for your *split-personality*
—i'm defective i think
like you
my childhood home was also bought & sold

—its walls have veins
a heart
& lungs to breathe life into bad dreams
—demons visit me in these strange reveries
like old friends
& they play vulgar theatre scenes
with *deep-rooted fears*
—everyday i lose a little bit of who i was
when i was with you
*i miss **her***
so i'm taking a break from normalcy today
i'm dead drunk & it's 3am
won't you send *all of hell* to stop me
please?
i'm visiting his grave
the one you often had to dial-up
when real life connections remained low
—i bet he tasted like rattlesnake-teeth
coated in
bong-flavoured vodka
—in your own words
you wished for his death
in a car crash in heat
—*you're not that person anymore*
—you still write love songs
but they have an undertone
of everything that is *mutated & sick*
—this crooked ghost you buried alive long ago
is worming his way back into your brain
—a tumour eating away what was *once* you
with his crooked teeth
& his crooked words
raping the english language
with a twisted head of his own
—*do i remind you of your youth?*
you feign sweetness
but you're a dosed needle in the hay
& when your voice grows shaky on the phone
amid pure ecstasy
it transports me back to a time
where you were in your *sexual prime*
my eyes threaten to *roll-back*

*along with nostalgia's trip
it's embarrassing really
—you're still a ranting tragedy
chronically online—
rare
bold &
beautiful
& filled to the brim with decay
funny*
but nothing compares to the carefully perceived persona
that is ~~you~~ *him*
him
*the video freak
the nose-
bleeding
stool-
sniffing
cokehead
the detestable*
creep
—twenty-twenty on fire flashing like dead stars
& overflowing with *diseased bleeding hearts*
—dying young was always the trend for him
but never for something as dead-end & modern
as *electric fame*
—today we live on ivs that pump sweet hate
—*racist hexes for the evil race*
—*sexist hexes for the evil sex*
—how would he hold me
with a good conscience in such a climate?
he's safe & frozen in electric dust now
in the shrine to your youth
—what would he do to me
in your dead time of sweet harmony
dipped in *utter* vulgarity?
your legacy is breathing life into a *sleaze*
—you loved setting art on fire & detesting
the whole world
but you couldn't do that without your *fake personality*
—for a *modern-day-him* reborn
i think i'd give up booze & fall into a dream coma
poison my breath with electric cigarettes by the hour
rot my teeth out of my head
with your *sickening-split-personality sweetness*...

This Ache Feels Like
someone is fine-dining on my battered insides, taking an impolite amount of time doing so. The ants, the flies, the butterflies, even the maggots are invited now and are working on eating the heart alive. My head - my brain, is now detached from the rest, it has grown far too tired and longs for common sense that the rest of the dying body no longer does possess. The body continues to crave living happily amid the suffering & the ache falls in love with me instead...

♡SUNLIGHT EATER♡

the only rose-coloured brain floating by starlight
drugged & painting a rebellion by 4 a.m. to 5.

kill me with your knife collection
show me a good time
—i'm your favorite dead-ant-farm
choking on your pain killers' regression.

i'm a joke as far as your fucked-off head bothers to label
it's a cheap price to pay
becoming a new online shrine
for you
because i'm looking to guillotine the hyphen
not fucking add to it...
did you have to force hands?
because you can't wait to cut off that part of yourself now
around me...

i'm the sugar bomb
melting your insides
only an hour a day.

please force monthly subscription self-help on me in return
ignore all my *real* feelings...
"drama queen"
it's written deep within my thighs
—*"piss drinking cunt"*
was the nicest thing you had ever called me
but don't think about touching me
not for a week.

what a power you possess

i'm overflowing with
jealous
hatred
in a night
—my hate choking on spite.

i won't play with what i respect
but i'm desperate to play.

chameleon
paying for perfect poses to copy
just to impress a heated text-message or two.

desert dream
cayenne for lips
we're the same.

you can refrigerate your blood on a dime
just like your maraschino cherries
—
& you steal the sun from me
you steal the sun from me
you steal the sun from me
anytime you promise something.

poem #37: July 2nd, 2018
"Piss Drinking Cunt"

I wonder if you'd throw me down,
and pound me like you wrote you would
such a mess on the wet, hard, cold
ground, the scent would be overbearing,
the scent of honey kisses, lavender,
rose water, piss and decaying, dark
wishes, your breaths would be as
heavy as rain clouds, before a
summer's storm in barely spring,
heavy with threats and promises and
taboo, vulgar little names,
I wonder if you could touch me
would you treat me so roughly?
dig your nails into my fleshy behind
and whisper possesive dreams
and remedies, would you finally
satiate this dark part of my
longing mind

♡List #5♡
Things You're Terrified To Write Down

1. _____
   _____
   _____
   _____

2. _____
   _____
   _____
   _____

3. _____
   _____
   _____
   _____

4. _____
   _____
   _____
   _____

5. _____
   _____
   _____
   _____

♡YOU'RE NEEDLE♡

special
when your body is no longer just yours
—your singing
voice is a pretentious drunk's idea of a rock dream *only*
you're needle
my mind is a pessimistic love record in pretend stupor
these words
are only here to secure a jealous future coated in *foreign sugar*
your words
are nervous vein heaters
you're weak
i'm drunken-turned on
but you can't let me see you choke on your own forced sweetener
garage floor show
you think you're winning me over
you're needle
i'm a passport
you're out of line most times
measured best as distracting poison in plastic *only*
you're foreign guilt shooting up veins where it doesn't belong
you're needle
i find i can only prematurely sleep on nights i'm meant to play with you
i don't care if we actually meet up on time
it always ends the same
sitting nervously
fun
but *nothing's cumming*
you're losing your blinding effect on me
but it's good to force the small talk instead of the *blade*
there's no good-consciousness today

only unconscious escapism with the shutters closed
alone
they call you pretty sometimes
but you only are for 2-seconds
no more
you're one drop more a dose any1 can stand
& you're loaded with hedonistic evidence
the only difference with you
is you're capable of *sharing it*
but the blood isn't truly just on your hands
you've got 7 years on me yet we sit in silence
in the exact same electric row boat
& on *my* nights only
i like you
yet no matter what you do
you won't manage to leave an almost invisible scar of your own
you won't manage to disappoint me to a
devastatingly *shaky* degree
like **he** could.

November 25th, 2018

I cannot relate 2 them, I cannot relate 2 them,
I cannot relate 2 them
I cannot relate 2 them
I cannot relate 2 them
I cannot relate 2 them

Send me 2 sleep...

♡THE CHERRY PIT♡

you say you'll be the reason i'm a picture of health
—*you know what you're talking about*
—you're a well-advised sleeping pill bottle
on late lonely saturday
that near-misses the same self-destructive
crimson-mess
that your own actions inflict on me.

the demons sheltering away from the sun
within my head
always seem to get their way without you near
—growing cherry-vines up behind my eyes
straight from the constant aching pit of hell
—*your forced-care demonstrating a convincing
disappearing act*
every friday.

i'm not gentle with myself on your ever-vacant watch
& when i play mean with my porcelain skin it's not pretend
& there's no aftercare
that has to be someone else's job in the end.

you're the warm bright blood of the sun when reality keeps
you engaged
—sizzling dead roadkill veins exposed in butterfly hearts
—i can't tear out the weeds you grew within your mind
—*i can't reach you or your remedies through your favourite
doctor this time.*

the sun slides down walls of brick
& solid rivers of black asphalt
for the fifth time this week
—remnants of blood-red cherries

still covering my fingertips & the tips of my crooked teeth
in another *pretty-mess*
sending me to my favourite rose-tinted dream in a pit so sweet
after a few.

you had said you'd be the reason i'll be a picture of health
—*you know what you're talking about*
you're a well-advised sleeping pill bottle on late nights
near-missing a *crimson-mess.*

yet friday nights you joyride around on motorcycles
itching to buy the luxardo cherries
that'll garnish your own alcoholic debauchery
& you'll throw the pits into the vacant ditch you dug for
yourself in a mere 5-years
deepening your dedicated relationship with death instead
on every weekend bender
you disappear...

♡HOSPITAL DRUGS♡

i don't like the way that you talk about death
—like a prayer
—like a wish
—like a sickness your body is distressingly tethered to yet obsessed with
—like something that'll happen within the week—
your sickness is a curse on our time—*your sickness is a lie*
—despite it all
i know you're an angel
because your vocal chords alone can strangle
pure hearts
& make evening spring breezes far sweeter to inhale
through bitterness
caused by *you*...
—i'll act like a child
sobbing—
tear-dried & magick obsessed—
picturing myself underneath your desk—kissing the angel on the shelf
while the moon poses as an uninvited guest—the same moon that spies on you too
getting high—what does it see?
—*soon*
chemicals will again trace the length of your imagined as sacred bloodstream—
forcing me selfish onto your mind in a sad drugged daze—
i practiced stranger's hedonism
while white walls
blank stares &
hospital chairs
pretended to be good company for you—
you so broken—
that i wait for—my heart disease is spoken for
by *you*—

78

everything you told me has always been *half-true*—
dreaming of those injected arms about my waist
still sends me reeling—
dreaming that if you were close enough to hold me
the cure would work its way down into you
through love's own warm sighs
like shockwaves

...or perhaps it'd make you worse.

I just thought, well a part of me did that he was lying about this sickness to use me.

Soon he stopped and said we were "experts at this" and claimed now there was a place in heaven for the perverse. He said he was expertly distracted when I had asked and said it was "weird/kinky/fucked up" to get excited in a hospital bed.

♡List #6♡
The Things That Keep You 'Alive'

1. _____
_____
_____
_____

2. _____
_____
_____
_____

3. _____
_____
_____
_____

4. _____
_____
_____
_____

5. _____
_____
_____
_____

♡DEADEND♡

i would live in a haunted house with you
haunting its innards to the brim
with our debauched memories instead
but you're a burning building all on your own
you'd break down every floor into nothing given the time
to fester & to think
—*a future aneurysm hiding in the brain.*

we met in unconsciousness
much too late
but your mind still held me anyway
through your warmer nights
& against the sick waves of sadness
that would crash upon the forefront of the brain
breaking on the rocky edges of our time.

i called you *"gorgeous"* & you must have thought it was a joke—
your brain fed off of mine
—said it was adoration
& taught me weed is sweet
death is divine
& hell lives on the streets in the form of
every other human mind
—you were the self-proclaimed optimist that
grew my own pessimism in the sun of your prettied words
pixelated
calculated
& funny.

i had a dream about your death
the midnight after your first wave of regret when it came to me
—ghosts would play house inside of me
& you were just another one living your life in my veins
overflowing every time i would speak
& your smoke signals would always float far
they'd die at heaven's door.

making you feel better was sweet polaroids & pressed cherry blossoms
taped into fresh morning journals
& lonely walks with your ghost presence spouting commands of confidence
—i pray you cut me off
because you're now nothing but a fully-realised disease
that i've had to live with for far too long
—i can't imagine myself without doing so through your own eyes first.

you had only said my name *twice*
sweetly-shakily as the telephone lines crossed
& the static grew *louder & louder* heating our imagination
until it sounded like steady rain
—*a storm*
on my hot december monday
lulling me back to peace & temporary release
—momentarily *happy* in *forced* funny drunken speech
—i remember we met in unconsciousness
much too late
i remember i arrived when you were wide awake & already
downing the *third* manhattan
on your warm alameda sunday
watching the tv shows that you *detest*
until your pretty windows had turned back into your head.

leave me only with wildfire veins & a microwave brain
in the dead of summer
allow me sleep in peace without having to pay for my dreams
—the humid stormy dawn always collecting the debt
—forced now to drown within your gasoline rain
all without the flame.

i'm lying in flowerbeds cutting out the pieces inside of me
that have long been rotting black
from once being touched by disembodied-desperate parts of you
—your excitement for me is now long-dried blood
on white bedsheets.

i'm done sharing my brain
but i would have lived in a haunted house with you
—i would have carved out the womb for glorified display
hopelessly dreaming of the day you'd look at my soul
& see a future with a heartbeat
rather than this dead-end carcass rotting in the sun
for all to see.

♡List #7♡
Looking Back, What Does The Small Word-Shrine You Have Built With These Lists Reveal About You?

1. _____
_____
_____
_____

2. _____
_____
_____
_____

3. _____
_____
_____
_____

4. _____
_____
_____
_____

5. _____
_____
_____
_____

♡FOREIGN GODS♡

it's as dead as the ocean is sometimes
after hours
in this empty bar where we talked for the first time
almost inaudibly
—your heart was brand new
posing as an overgrown garden maze for me to play
carve & change
—heavy waves crashed forcibly against the grand
windows all around
revealing our secret meeting to the endless blackness of a
storm
making us lightheaded
& sickeningly nervous
even more
—sea salt on the glass
eating time away
—the screaming wind
—whirlwind of eating feelings inside of me
& i was alone again
but this silent ship was slowly overflowing
with brand new lusty schemes
just to have you
mixed like poison within the warm blood circulating
around the briefly-buzzed brain
—experimenting with tenderness
—i was once like an island
unmoving
unchanging
—cold waterfall veins cutting across mountains of
untouched bone & flesh
—looking you in the eyes was like looking into hell
for the first time
—numb with curiosity
frozen with the fear of some dreamy

brand new beginning magically sent
to further drain my life for me
—*reverse iv*
—the reckless kind of excitement you feel far from home
lost in a thunderstorm
& while throwing up in the street in front of rowdy
strangers alone
—i'd tell you about my strange days later on the phone
—*my brand new morning ritual*
talking about the weather with foreign gods who live by
the ocean

where i now meet **you**. . .